Windmill Books and E. P. Dutton
New York

# The Voyage of OSIRIS · *A Myth of Ancient Egypt*

## retold and illustrated by Gerald McDermott

## About the Artist

Gerald McDermott was born in Detroit. He studied at the Detroit Institute of Arts and was awarded a scholarship to Pratt Institute. In New York, McDermott pursued a dual interest in graphics and film making. He produced a series of animated films on folklore and mythology that brought him international recognition. McDermott's beautifully illustrated books are an organic outgrowth of his fascination with myth.

*Anansi the Spider*, a Caldecott Honor Book and *Arrow to the Sun*, Caldecott Medal winner established McDermott as one of the foremost graphic interpreters of mythological themes.

*The Voyage of Osiris* is McDermott's most complex and subtle work. His striking development is manifest in the luminous color and elegant imagery he has brought to a ritual drama over 5,000 years old.

## About the Book

The art work for this book was rendered with opaque watercolors on 300 lb. watercolor paper, handmade in the Sri Aurobindo Ashram, in Pondicherry, India. The art was reproduced in five colors.

The text type is 18 point Alpha Palatino. The book was printed on 80 lb. Paloma matte by offset and is bound in cloth over boards. The binding is reinforced and side-sewn.

## Selected Bibliography

Budge, E. A. Wallace. *The Gods of the Egyptians* 2 vols. New York. Dover Publications (reprint), 1969

_____*Osiris and the Egyptian Resurrection*. 2 vols. New York. Dover Publications (reprint), 1973

Campbell, Joseph. *The Hero with a Thousand Faces*. Princeton. Bollingen University Press, 1972

Frazer, Sir James G. *The Golden Bough*. New York. Macmillan Company, 1971 (See especially chapters 38-42)

Scott, Nora. *The Daily Life of the Ancient Egyptians*. New York. Publication of the Metropolitan Museum of Art, undated.

Seele, Keith C., and Steindorff, George. *When Egypt Ruled the East*. Chicago. Chicago University Press, 1957

Wolff, Walther. *The Origins of Western Art*. New York. Universe Books, 1971

Copyright © 1977 by Gerald McDermott
All rights reserved
Published by Windmill Books & E. P. Dutton
201 Park Avenue South, New York, New York 10003

Published simultaneously in Canada by Clarke, Irwin & Company, Limited, Toronto and Vancouver
Edited by Robert Kraus
Designed by Jane Byers Bierhorst
Typography by The Royal Composing Room
Printing by Universal Printing Company
Binding by Book Press
Produced by David Zable
Printed in the U.S.A. First Edition
10 9 8 7 6 5 4 3 2 1

*Library of Congress Cataloging in Publication Data*

McDermott, Gerald.
The Voyage of Osiris, a myth of ancient Egypt

1. Osiris—Juvenile literature. 2. Isis—Juvenile literature. [1. Osiris. 2. Isis. 3. Mythology, Egyptian] I. Title.
PZ8.1.M159Vo        [E]            77-2861
ISBN: 0-525-61567-9

*For the Isis of the Shepaug*

siris, the Green One,
Osiris, Beloved Pharaoh, Osiris, Molder of Civilization.

He instructs us in the arts. He teaches us to make the delta green with fruit trees and grape vines.

Isis, his wife and sister, Isis, giver of wheat and barley, Isis, the Throne.

Osiris and Isis, together they give life to Egypt, together they rule in peace.

While Isis governs wisely, Osiris travels over the earth, sowing the seeds of knowledge.

Osiris returns to Egypt in triumph, crowned with the garlands of far-off lands.

He is feted by his evil brother, Set, the animal-headed one, who covets the Pharaoh's throne.

The wretched Set traps Osiris. At a banquet, he brings forth a large chest, worked in gold and many colors. Set invites each guest to lie down in the chest; he who fits shall have the magnificent coffer.

When Osiris obliges, Set and his conspirators rush forward, slamming down the lid of the coffin. Set seals the chest with his burning breath.

He casts the chest into the Nile and Osiris is carried out to sea.

Set ascends to the throne.

Isis flees and takes refuge in the papyrus swamps, guarded by seven scorpions.

She floods the Nile with her tears.

The precious coffer containing Osiris washes ashore in Byblos. A giant sycamore tree grows up around the chest, enfolds and swallows it.

The King of Byblos admires this beautiful tree. He commands that the tree be cut down and carved into a huge column for his palace. The king does not know that Osiris is sealed within.

Isis journeys to Byblos to be near Osiris.
She becomes a nursemaid in the royal household.
   While the palace sleeps, Isis changes into a swallow
and flies mournfully round the pillar that conceals
her husband.
   One night, the queen rushes into the chamber, drawn by
cries of her unattended child.

Isis is startled in mid-flight and her spell is broken. She reveals herself and pleads that she be given the coffin of Osiris.

This is granted and the chest is carved out of the heart of the sycamore column.

Isis sails for Egypt. During the voyage, she hovers
over Osiris in the form of a hawk and conceives a child.

When Isis reaches Egypt she hides the precious coffer
of Osiris in the marshes. She gives birth to their
hawk-headed son, Horus.

During a moonlight hunt for wild boar, Set comes upon the coffer. He realizes it is Osiris and smashes the chest to bits. Set cuts Osiris into pieces and casts them to the wind.

Isis, with her son and sister, roams painfully over the desert, gathering the broken body of Osiris.

Weeping and moaning with grief, they tenderly bind him together with endless lengths of fine linen.

Overhead, the Sun-God Ra hears their lamentations and halts his solar boat.

Ra pities the mourning Isis. He sends ibis-headed
Thoth, Keeper of Wisdom, and jackal-headed Anubis,
Guardian of the Dead, to help. Thoth touches the lips
of Osiris with the Sign of Life.

All gather round and through their magic powers
raise Osiris up to dwell in the West, to reign again as
Lord of the Underworld.

We gaze once more upon the gracious face of Osiris and rejoice. Now all will journey from this earth to live again in the realm of Osiris.